MAKE MONEY TEACHING COOKING CLASSES

A Guide to Start Your Own Kids Cooking Business

By Kathe Hamilton and Kery Jackson

Founders of the popular kids cooking school

Dedication

To Mom and Dad, our angels in
heaven that have guided us in spirit
every step of the way.

Table of Contents

Introduction

Dad's German Chocolate Cake, Mom's Coconut Pineapple Cake, and The Kids' Yellow Cake with Chocolate Icing, these were the cakes our Mom would make every Christmas Eve. We all got our favorites and the best part was licking the batter off the mixing beaters and bowl. Cooking meant family, love, laughter, memories and traditions. We grew up loving good food and sharing it with family and friends so when it was time to focus on a potential business venture, it was not hard to agree on cooking and sharing our love of cooking with children. We always wanted to start a business but there never seemed to be the right time. We would talk, write down ideas and "dream" but we were not sure when we would start.

Everything Happens for a Reason

Sometimes it is the unexpected things that push you to follow your dreams. Unfortunately, for us it was the passing of our mother on April 30, 2008. Both of our parents died before the age of 65 and never got to enjoy retirement. Our mother's death was especially life altering for us. It had been so unexpected and it really made us reflect on the important things in life. We decided that we would not wait any longer to pursue our passions. We started by meeting every weekend to discuss what we wanted to do. We made a list of all the things that we loved and all the things that we were good at. We were both teachers so our interests were very similar. We both enjoyed working with kids, crafts, cooking, and entertaining. Being moms ourselves, we understood the needs of working mothers. Most of the things that we listed were primarily kid-focused activities. We started searching the Internet and came across a variety of concepts. One thing we learned is that just about everything we thought of was already out there! From kids hair salons to mobile birthday party services! We learned that our ideas were not unique but we felt that our expertise and our approach to business would make us stand out among the rest. Somehow we knew it would be all about our level of commitment and our vision.

Vision and Commitment

It may sound corny but Vision Boards do work! My sister had just heard about them from The Oprah Show. I knew a little bit about them but had never tried making one. Our first one was very simple. It was just chart paper and markers. We drew pictures of what we wanted for our business. First we drew our cooking shop storefront, then our unique sign of our logo on the building and finally, pictures of many children learning to cook. We knew we wanted to focus on what we were passionate about. We were family, there was trust, and we worked well together.

Most importantly, we had the same vision and level of commitment. We emphasized our strengths and experience with children to integrate cooking and academic skills such as math, science, measurement, and reading. By the spring, we decide to focus on our cooking and trying a few things at home with our own children and with our family and friends. It was a success! Our family and friends were eager to come back for the next cooking class. Before we knew it our ideas had turned into a real plan and The Kids' Cooking Place was born! This was not our first choice as a name for our business but we will discuss that later when we talk about a little thing called trademark.

The "Lucy and Ethel" Approach to Business

My sister and I grew up in the 70's watching a small black and white TV with about five channels to choose from for our entertainment. Some of our fondest memories were watching shows like: *I Love Lucy, What's Happening,* and so many more. When we decided to start our business, we often felt like Lucy and Ethel opening a dress shop, selling salad dressing or making chocolates in a factory. Sometimes we had wild ideas and just ran with it and laughed along the way whether it worked or not. So just remember to have fun and don't sweat the small stuff.

We certainly learned a lot on our journey to follow our dreams and open our business. Some things were good, some not so good, but we did it and you can do it too!! Our goal is to share all the things we learned so you can do it even better. I guess what we know for sure is that we will always be educators at heart and we hope you learn from our lessons on the journey to success. Enjoy!

The Business Plan/ Trademarks

No clue? Pay someone to do it for you!

A **business plan** is a formal document detailing the goals that the business will have. It will also include how the goals will be met, cash resources, and the people involved with the company. Most plans cover the first 3-5 years of the business. Business plans should be updated about every 5 years.

For a home-based or mobile cooking business, you can create a business plan in 30-60 minutes with a simple fill-in the blank template available on various websites.

If you are planning to be in a retail space, I strongly recommend paying a company to do a very strategic and tactical business plan for the most detailed projection of your business.

We used www.businessplans.com for $385. Their service provided us with a 20-25 page professional plan within about 3 days. Prices vary but expect to pay about $250 and up, but it's worth the breakdown and analysis of information you get in return.

Additional websites that create business plans:
- www.FormSwift.com
- www.enloop.com
- www.planware.org

A **trademark** is a proprietary term that is usually registered with the Patent and Trademark Office to assure its exclusive use by its owner. A trademark basically protects your brand name or logo. We created and designed our own brand name and logo and felt that we wanted to protect it in case we ever decide to franchise our business. We originally called our business *Kids R Cooking*, but soon learned from our trademark attorney that a well known toy company that uses a single "R" in their logo would probably not let us use it. So we changed our name to avoid any legal issues.

I suggest you weigh the pros and cons of whether you want to trademark your brand name or logo. But also make a decision <u>before</u> starting your business. We made a very costly mistake of having signs and merchandise created with our original *Kids R Cooking* logo that we could no longer use.

(This was our second sign after changing our name)

Financing

"Show me the money!"

If you work full-time and need to keep your job while you pursue your entreprencurial dreams, no problem. We did the same thing. Later when your business starts to make a profit you may consider working part-time or hopefully saying good-bye to your 9-5 completely! Also, consider developing another stream of income to cover the initial costs of starting your own business.

Examples of possible ways to earn a little extra income:

* Tutoring at home
* Selling baked goods from home
* Running errands for busy parents and the elderly
* Doing one-on-one cooking classes/private cook
* Catering small events
* Party planning
* Doing market research surveys ($50-$150 paid for each survey for kids or adults)

Survey companies I have used:
www.trotta.net
www.aimresearchnetwork.com
* Something new out there for fundraising is
www.gofundme.com

You may need to cutback or reduce expenses by:

* Pay-off credit cards
* Cheaper phone plans or bundle plans
* Change or cancel extra cable channels/ plans
* Try to lower interest rates

Borrow or barter for money or services (just suggestions):

* Refinancing a home or car
* Taking a line of credit
* Borrowing from retirement funds or life insurance policies
* Apply for small business loans www.sba.gov
* Stay in touch with a good plumber, electrician, painter, etc… you will definitely need them if you chose to have a retail space for your business.

* (You may be able to exchange cooking lessons for their services. Can't hurt to ask.)

Don't be afraid to tell the world what you're planning or what you need

* Use every kind of social media there is to get the word out.
* Extended friends and family
* Talk to people at the post office, grocery store, schools, beauty shop etc…

You'd be surprised how many strangers have said they were interested in our business when we mentioned it. You might find a like-minded person to invest in your business.

*Bonus Suggestion: The secret to getting a large credit line quickly, Shhh!!!

Okay so a friend who has been in business for several years gave me this monumental advice when starting your own business. I think this was the best advice we have ever received to this day!

If you have pretty good credit, you should be able to get several personal and business credit cards with limits as high as $2000-$4000 on each card.

The trick is… you must apply for all of the credit cards you want **IN ONE DAY**! Why? It will only ding your credit for that one day versus 10 credit companies checking your credit over and over again on different days.

We tried this and we were able to get about 7 new credit cards in one day. Some with our LLC business name, some with just our personal names. In an instant, we had over **$10,000** to start our own business!!!

(Reminder this is a suggestion. Be prepared to **pay** your monthly fees to your creditors every month.)

Just having this cushion of money to buy big ticket items from places like Home Depot or Lowes was a huge help. We had to build a kitchen for our retail space. Luckily, we were able to buy a refrigerator, stove, dishwasher and many more essential items that were required to have a full kitchen by using these credit cards. The space we rented only had the walls, a bathroom and a concrete floor. It was crucial to use the funds to transform the cold space into a cozy kid-friendly cooking atmosphere.

(We found a reasonable painter from talking to the beauty salon owner next to our store.)

Estimated Start-Up Costs

"Yes, You CAN!"

It's important to set an estimated limit to how much you will spend before you open up for business. The amount of your overhead is the major factor in the costs to start-up.

Home-based cooking business:

* Start-up costs, about $3000

Mobile cooking business:

* Start-up costs, about $7,000

Retail space cooking business (with a full kitchen):

* Start-up costs, about $30,000

Our business start-up costs for opening in a retail space was about $60,000. Monthly rent and any structural updates needed in the facility make a <u>huge</u> difference. The retail space we rented had <u>no kitchen, no gas, and</u>

<u>concrete floors.</u> The majority of our start-up costs went to building a full kitchen, plumbing, electrical rewiring and flooring.

I highly recommend you rent a space that already has a full kitchen!

Now if it doesn't have a full kitchen, don't throw in the towel. Everything does not have to be purchased at once. Buy the most important items first. Designate items that will be purchased with a <u>portion</u> of each paycheck, savings, or credit card each month. Once you start making small commitments to purchase items for your business, this will fuel your momentum to see it through to the end.

(This was our kitchen in the making. We had to add special electrical outlets.)

Appliances/Kitchen Supplies/Furniture

$hop-a-holics beware

Home-Based Cooking Business

* **A good reliable oven. Gas or electric.** (Preferably a double oven for cooking main dishes and desserts at the same time.)
* Measure the size of your oven before buying sheet pans/cookie sheets. There are some sheet pans that don't fit inside of a regular kitchen oven.
* Dishwashers are definitely a plus.
* **Sturdy** fold-up tables and chairs are a must have. Try Costco, Sam's Club etc… for the best quality and prices. You probably don't want your students cutting on your nice kitchen/dining room tables.
* Basic kitchen appliances: 2-3 hand mixers, blenders, microwave, electric griddle, crockpot, pasta maker, apple peeler etc… depending on your recipes.

* Sturdy dishwasher safe/microwaveable plastic plates, bowls, cups, and chopping mats. We used the colorful ones from IKEA. They are very sturdy.
* Lettuce knives (All plastic, no metal/blade.) About $2-$5 each. Kids can chop, slice, and dice without the worry of a sharp blade. Limited supply at grocery stores, TJ Maxx/Home Goods, and try various kitchen supply stores.
* *A few websites we came across: www.amazon.com , www.oxo.com.*
* 1-2 file cabinets for keeping all your documents organized.
* Basic miscellaneous kitchen supplies: Stainless steel mixing bowls, pots/pans, several sets of measuring cups/spoons (for wet/dry ingredients), parchment paper (must have for easy clean-up), and much more as needed! **I suggest you buy from a restaurant/chef supply store or Costco Business store for one-stop shopping.**

(You can provide small cooking parties at
your home or in the client's home.)

Mobile Cooking Business

* **A reliable SUV/Truck/Van is crucial** for
  storage of ALL your supplies. Depending
  on the kind of cooking business service
  you are providing to your customers.
* Your vehicle is your mobile office, mobile
  kitchen and your livelihood. Make sure
  you pack **everything** you may need in
  your car, plus extra.
* Decide if you are providing tables, chairs,
  portable ovens etc… or will you be using

the customers? We tried both ways. We used a homeowner's oven and chairs for a birthday party and we provided the fold-up tables. That worked out nicely, but we felt a little in the way when using her oven. Party food needed to be warmed up at the same time.

* Also every oven cooks differently. If possible, I suggest using a portable toaster oven or hot plate for small birthday parties. (Wal-Mart, Big Lots and Target have decent prices)

* Get a **magnetic sign to advertise** your business **on your car**.

* **Sturdy** fold-up tables and chairs are a must have. Try Costco, Sam's Club etc… for the best quality and prices. You probably don't want your students cutting on someone's nice kitchen/dining room tables.

* Basic kitchen appliances: 2-3 hand mixers, blenders, microwave, electric griddle, crockpot, pasta maker, apple peeler etc… depending on your recipes.

* Sturdy dishwasher safe/microwaveable plastic plates, bowls, cups, and chopping

mats. We used the colorful ones from IKEA. They are very sturdy.

* Lettuce knives (All plastic, no metal/ blade.) About $2-$5 each. Kids can chop, slice, and dice without the worry of a sharp blade. Limited supply at grocery stores, TJ Maxx/Home Goods, and try various kitchen supply stores.

* *A few websites we came across: www.amazon.com , www.oxo.com.*

* 1-2 file cabinets for keeping all your documents organized.

* Basic miscellaneous kitchen supplies: Stainless steel mixing bowls, pots/pans, several sets of measuring cups/spoons (for wet/dry ingredients), parchment paper (must have for easy clean-up), and much more as needed! **I suggest you buy from a restaurant/chef supply store or Costco Business store for one-stop shopping.**

Retail Space Cooking Business

* A good reliable oven. Gas or electric.
  (Preferably a double oven for cooking
  main dishes and desserts at the same time.)
* Large-sized refrigerator with freezer.
* Three compartment sink. (check with
  codes/permits for your state)
* Measure the size of your oven before
  buying sheet pans/cookie sheets. There are
  some sheet pans that don't fit inside of a
  regular kitchen oven.
* Dishwashers are definitely a plus, but may
  require a separate permit. Check with the
  codes for your state on adding major
  appliances. We bought a dishwasher and
  later found out that it would require us to
  apply for an additional permit just to have
  it installed. Needless to say, we never had
  it installed because it would have taken
  another 3-6 weeks to get approved for this
  permit.
* Basic kitchen appliances: 4-5 hand mixers,
  1-2 blenders, microwave, electric griddle,

crockpot, pasta maker, apple peeler etc…
depending on your recipes.
* Sturdy dishwasher safe/microwaveable
plastic plates, bowls, cups, and chopping
mats. We used the colorful ones from
IKEA. They are very sturdy.
* Lettuce knives (All plastic, no metal/
blade.) About $2-$5 each. Kids can chop,
slice, and dice without the worry of a
sharp blade. Limited supply at grocery
stores, TJ Maxx/Home Goods, and try
various kitchen supply stores.
A few websites we came across:
www.amazon.com , www.oxo.com.
* 1-2 file cabinets for keeping all your
documents organized.
* Basic miscellaneous kitchen supplies:
Stainless steel mixing bowls, pots/pans,
several sets of measuring cups/spoons (for
wet/dry ingredients), parchment paper
(must have for easy clean-up), and much
more as needed! **I suggest you buy from
a restaurant/chef supply store or Costco
Business store for one-stop shopping.**

(This was our finished kitchen.)

Retail Space ~Furniture and Room set-up

The style of furniture and room set-up for a retail space is a personal choice. These are just some suggestions that you may find helpful when setting up your retail space.

* 1-2 office desks/chairs

* 1-2 file cabinets for keeping all your documents organized.

* 4-5 Shelves for merchandise display, storage, supplies etc…

* 5-6 Student work area tables (stainless steel, butcher block, granite etc…) you should be able to fit 6-8 students at each table for cooking classes and parties. (Rectangle shapes worked well for us)

* 20-25 sturdy chairs that can be wiped clean. We found very sturdy plastic stackable chairs at IKEA. (No fabric, no leather etc…)

Optional: couch or benches for parents observing and adult party guests.

Your set-up should allow for an easy walk flow from each area in your retail space. Consider the location of your bathroom, stove, and front door.

(Set-up for small cooking class or event.)

Site Selection

Location, Location, Location!

Just like with any real estate venture, location is the key. This kind of business is providing a service that is operating primarily during after-school hours and weekends. Consider the group of people in that area that would have the ability to pay for your service. Your business plan should give you a breakdown of the demographics in the area that you plan to open your business.

Scout around the area you are interested in for similar kid-focused businesses. Check their age groups, prices, hours, and number of participants. (Examples: karate, dance, art, music, tutoring, YMCA's etc…)

<u>Zoning, Parking, and Permits</u>

"The Stickiest Red Tape Ever"

Your due diligence will be the bulk of your time, energy, and headache medicine. **Due diligence** is an investigation of a business or person prior to signing a contract, or an act with a certain standard of care. Usually it takes about 30 days to get as much information as possible before you sign a lease on a retail space. For example, we were required to put down a deposit to the landlord while we did our due diligence. This ensured us that he could not rent the space to someone else during those 30 days.

Zoning describes the control by authority of the use of land, and the buildings thereon. Every city and state has their own rules and regulations when it comes to this area. So check zoning rules first. If you plan to have a home-based cooking business, zoning maybe a little bit tricky. You may need a homeowner's association approval or other community approvals due to this being a private residence. Neighbors may not want a steady stream of strangers coming to their area every week.

For a retail space cooking business, zoning is a little easier. Most retail spaces are zoned for several types of businesses. For example, our retail space was zoned like a child care facility. We were lucky that no additional parking was required to change from its existing office space to a child care facility. Parking is the one that's trickier. You have to have enough parking for when you have parties. No one wants to park a mile away to go to a kid's birthday party. Also in a retail space, you usually have to share a parking lot with other businesses.

You should find out the hours of operation for all the businesses that may compete with your business for parking. If you choose to provide parties or special events, your high need for parking spaces will be on Saturday and Sunday afternoons.

Health Permits authorize a person to operate a food facility. All food facilities that store, prepare, package, serve, vend, or otherwise provide food and beverage for human consumption at a retail level or wholesale must have a valid health permit. These laws have changed since we started our business. Again, every city and state has their own rules. Check with your local city Health Department laws before getting started with your business. Many states now allow health permits to cook and sell products out of your own home kitchens.

Our biggest hurdle was getting clearance from the Health Department for our retail space. We had to prove to them that we did not need a commercial kitchen to have a cooking school. Our argument was that we were not selling food. Our students were making the food and eating it there. We finally convinced the health department that a commercial kitchen was not required for a cooking business, unless you plan to **sell** food. This decision was the yay or nay of us opening our business. Building a commercial kitchen would have cost us an extra $15,000-$50,000.

Lease Negotiations
"It's just like buying a car"

Do your homework or enlist the help of someone who understands real estate and leasing property. Your overhead is the biggest expense with almost any business.

For the home-based and mobile cooking business, this shouldn't be an issue since you're operating from your home or car.

A retail space cooking business will need to either buy or lease a building. A **lease** has a set term, during which the tenant agrees to rent the property. Leases are suitable for landlords who want to "lock in" a tenant for a set period of time. Most new businesses agree to a 2-5 year term lease with an option to extend. Choose a comfortable amount of time that you feel you can commit to. Ask the buildings nearby how much they are paying for rent and how long is their lease? Pay close attention to *common area* *operating expenses, rent increases, required insurance, property or sewage taxes, subleasing, signage restrictions* and additional expenses that might be listed on your lease agreement.

(This optimal location was our first choice, but negotiations fell through…it was a blessing in disguise.)

Vendors and Merchandise

"Seek and you shall find"

You will need to do a little price comparison shopping in order to get the best deals for your consumable supplies and merchandise. Buying wholesale is typical for most businesses. **Wholesale** is the selling of goods in large quantities to be retailed by others. Get the necessary tax documents and licenses in order to buy items at the wholesale price. Wholesale distributors will only sell their products to established businesses.

Most states require you to get a federal tax ID, also known as an Employer Identification Number (EIN) and/or license. The forms and applications are online from the IRS.gov website.

Some of the things you will need to buy in large quantities are:

*Aprons, chef hats
*Paper goods, parchment paper, foil/plastic wraps
*Food (mainly pantry items like flour, sugar, oil etc…)
*Bathroom supplies
*Cleaning supplies

Figure out how much you need **before** you go shopping. Don't over buy! You need to consider where you will store all those bulk items and how much will you use before it expires.

Here are a few suggestions of places that might have better deals or sell products wholesale:

*Costco/Sam's Club or any membership card warehouse store in your area.
*Restaurant supply stores and depots.
*Chef supply stores
* www.growingcooks.com (Best deals for aprons, hats, etc…)

Buying **merchandise** to sell with your business is optional, but it's also a simple way to make some extra cash. Whether you're cooking business is home-based, mobile, or a retail store having something to sell allows your customers an opportunity to purchase some of the products that you might use in your cooking classes. You can also sell them on your website to reach even more customers.

I recommend selling merchandise that is **very unique, adult and kid-friendly and make good gifts**. Checkout cooking trade shows, farmers markets, and swap meets for great ideas. For example, we displayed hand-made aprons from a local grandmother in our area. We worked out a deal to showcase her aprons in our store window for just a small percentage of the profits, if they sold.

Here are some suggestions of the kinds of merchandise that you can sell:

Fabric aprons (with and without your logo)
Chef hats
Cooking mitts
Cooking utensils (especially kid-friendly and bright colors)
Baking pans/pots
Cookbooks
Storybooks about food
Lunch pails/bags
Cooking kits
Cooking play sets
Cooking games
Cooking videos/DVDs
Gift baskets (offer custom-made for special events too)

1st Year Expenses

Blow the dust off your wallets

This is **just an example** of the possible 1st year expenses for a cooking business. Expenses vary depending on fees/prices in your city. Of course if you have a home-based or mobile cooking business, some of these expenses will not apply to you.

*Rent
*Contractor fees (depends on specific needs)
*Legal fees (Forming an L.L.C, contracts & trademark attorney)
*License/Permits
*Maintenance/Repairs (depends on the condition of the space)
*Bank account fees
*Payroll costs
*Credit card machine fees
*Credit protection plan
*Credit card payments
*Insurance
*Telephone/Internet/Cell phone
*Printing costs
*Postage

*Merchandise
*Travel
*Business meals
*Office supplies
*Cooking supplies/Appliances
*Inventory
*Memberships (warehouse stores, small business clubs)
*Signage (keep it simple to start off)
*Website hosting/domain names
*Logo design (Trademarks can be expensive)
*Advertising/marketing

Marketing and Advertising

"Get in the game"

A large chunk of your start-up costs will focus on marketing and advertising. **Marketing** is knowing who your existing or potential buyers are for your specific goods or services. Who is your target audience?

Here are the people and places to target for potential customers:

* Middle/Upper class level families (depending on how you set your prices)
* Women, Mothers, Stay at home moms/ dads
* Home school groups, group homes for kids
* Girl/Boy scouts (many need to earn their cooking badge)
* Mommy and me groups/clubs
* Local schools/daycares/camps (offer field trips, workshops or discounts for large groups)

* YMCA's , Boys and Girls clubs, After-school programs (especially for a mobile cooking business)
* Churches
* Restaurants
* Specialty stores/markets (health food markets, cooking supply stores)
* Bakeries
* Farmer's markets
* Libraries
* Trade shows
* Culinary schools/chef academies/colleges
* County fairs/baking competitions

Set-up informational tables and/or offer a free demonstration class whenever possible. Some places might require a vendor fee or temporary permit for their location. Don't blow your budget on being a vendor at expensive conventions and major trade shows. You're probably not ready for that unless you have a few hundred dollars to spare. I suggest going to smaller trade shows that are kid-focused, cook-off competitions or women's boutique/pamper shows. Anywhere there might be a group of women or kids walking around ready to buy something!

Advertising is the act or practice of calling attention to one's product, service, need, etc. There are many ways to advertise your business. The least expensive is by word of mouth. Good news travels fast, but you need to advertise in more than one way to reach potential customers.

Here are some popular ways to advertise:

* Every social media site, blog, or email blast
* Local newspapers
* Parent/Children's magazines
* Local radio or television commercials
* Billboards, bus stop benches, posters
* Flyers, door hangs, postcards, business card (drop-offs in your area)
* Join professional business groups and network (you might cross advertise with another local business)
* Magnetic signs on your car

Advertising is an on-going cost. You should **never stop advertising.** You might consider setting up 6-12 month contracts with newspaper and magazine ads for a better price. Also, when customers begin to call to inquire about your business, ask them how they learned about your business. This will help you know which ads are giving you the most traffic. Having a **website** for your business is also an on-going cost, but necessary.

Setting up your website can be very overwhelming. Browse other business websites and see which styles you like. Check out some food websites and other cooking businesses to get some ideas. Most websites will have the website company at the bottom of the homepage. Contact the company for a quote on setting-up your website. You might also consider creating your own website. Of course it will be a lot cheaper, but perhaps less professional looking. There are a few companies that do most or all of the work for you like www.godaddy.com or www.vistaprint.com.

Another cool company to consider is www.constantcontact.com. It's a feature that you add to your website to keep track of who is visiting your website.

(This was one of our most popular advertisements.)

Planning and Organizing

Becoming an entrepreneur!

It starts with having a very strategic and tactical business plan that I suggested in the section of this book on *The Business Plan*. Reminder try (www.businessplans.com).

Planning your cooking business begins with knowing your objectives for starting the business in the first place. If it's to make a million dollars, I'm afraid you will be disappointed with this business or any other business if money is your sole reason for becoming an entrepreneur. Opening your business is not all about you trying get as much money as possible from your customers.

Your objective for starting a business should be closely aligned with your mission statement. Think about what kind of role model you represent to your potential customers. What do you want to develop or increase with this cooking business? What do you want your customers to gain from patronizing your business? What can you offer that sets you apart from other businesses? Once you are able to verbalize and visualize your dreams/goals, then you and others will see the value that your business serves.

Now, with that said here are some suggestions for the types of sales literature you may need. Your sales literature should be able to answer the questions of who, what, when, where and why of the services your company is providing.

- History/bio/about us information on the owners and/or company.
- Services offered (classes, parties, workshops etc…)
- Prices
- Employees
- Schedules or hours of operation
- Press release
- Brochures, business cards, flyers etc…

Organize your business so that you and your employees will be in a state of mental competence to perform your services successfully! Organizing and planning go hand-in-hand. Once you have made your plans on how you want your cooking business to run, now organize everything in an accessible file, box, or shelf.

File:(1-2 file cabinets are a must have to stay organized)

> * Copies of recipes
> * Brochures, flyers, postcards
> ⁕ Calendar/schedule of classes, parties
> * Party information, registration forms
> * Sign in/out forms for classes or camps
> * Copies of contracts, permits, licenses, legal papers
> * Vendor papers, invoices, order forms, receipts
> * Bank accounts, credit card accounts, taxes, payroll accounts

Shelf:(You need at least 2-4 shelves: 1-2 for your personal use and 1-2 for displaying merchandise to sell. Something sturdy but still looks nice)

> * Cookbooks, storybooks, cd's
> * DVD's, kitchen toys
> * All merchandise

Boxes:(use see-through boxes and label them)

> * Party supplies, decorations, crayons/markers/pencils
> * Extra cooking supplies, aprons, chef hats
> * Cleaning materials, bathroom supplies

(Merchandise for sell on an IKEA shelf.)

Parties/Classes/Workshops

"Let the good times roll!"

This is actually the easiest part! Children and parents will already be excited for their event and eager to have fun with their friends while cooking at the same time. As long as you and your staff are trained well in working with children and stay on schedule, this will be a piece of cake!

Here are the main points to remember whether you are doing a party, class, or workshop. I call them the 4 C's.

Clock- Timing is everything. You must start on time and finish on time. You need enough time in between events to clean-up/set-up for the next party, class, or workshop. You do not want to compromise your next client's time because you were not ready. This sets a bad reputation for your business. You're only getting paid for the time that the customer agreed to in their contract. Why work longer but not get paid for it?

Check- Throughout the party, you will need to check the food in the oven, check for clean bathroom/spills and check the clock to stay on schedule.

Control- You or your staff must stay in control of the event, the children, and the parents. Enforce the rules to the children and the parents about running, taking turns, and appropriate behavior during your event. **Every parent is different**. Very often, if you don't say anything about requiring appropriate behavior… the parents will ignore disruptive behavior and your event will quickly get out of control.

Captivate- Think of yourself as a Master of Ceremonies, comedian, magician, TEACHER etc… You will need to maintain the attention of your clients for 1 1/2 to 2 hrs. You want them entertained and excited about every step of their cooking

experience. I suggest giving interesting facts about what they are cooking, tell personal stories, jokes, ask them questions, read picture books during transition times, or play food related games.

Kid-Friendly Recipes, Tips and More!

Here are a few of our popular kid-friendly recipes to get you started.

Appetizer:

Mango Salsa

2 medium chopped tomatoes, 1 chopped mango,
¼ cup chopped green bell pepper, ¼ cup chopped red onion
1 tsp. garlic, 1 tbsp. olive oil, juice of ½ a large lime
1/8 cup fresh cilantro leaves, chopped
Salt and black pepper to taste
Mix all together in a small mixing bowl and serve.

Entree:
Chicken Enchiladas

2 cups of chopped cooked chicken, a 16 oz
can of enchilada sauce, 2 green onions
chopped,
½ cup of a brown onion chopped, 6 corn or
flour tortillas,
2 cups shredded cheddar cheese, black
olives (optional).
Dip each tortilla in the sauce and put about a
tablespoon of chicken and cheese and
a sprinkle of brown onions inside each
tortilla.
Then, roll up the tortillas and place them in a
baking dish. Pour more sauce on top.
Next, sprinkle with cheese, green onions,
and olives. Bake at 450 F for about 20-25
minutes.

Flour Tortilla Recipe

* 2 cups all purpose flour
* 1/4 cup vegetable shortening, cut into
pieces
* 1/2 tsp. salt
* 1/2 tsp. baking powder
* 3/4 cup warm water

1. In a bowl, blend flour, salt, baking powder and shortening until it resembles fine meal.

2. Add warm water, a little at a time, to flour mixture and toss until liquid is incorporated. Water amount will vary with different flour types.

3. Form dough into a ball and kneed on a floured surface until dough is smooth and elastic. Divide, and make 12 smaller balls. Cover and let stand at least 30 minutes.

Cooking Tortilla:
4. Roll each ball of dough on a floured surface to make 6 or 7 inch sized tortillas. Place on a pre-heated griddle or cast iron skillet and cook till medium golden on both sides.

5. Remove to a basket lined with a cloth towel or put between towels until cool. After the tortillas have cooled completely, store them in a plastic bag. This recipe will make approximately 12 flour tortillas.

<u>Dessert:</u>

Churro Recipe

Makes about 2 dozen, 4 inch churros

*1 cup water

*2 Tbs brown sugar

*1/2 tsp. salt

*1/3 cup butter

*1 cup white flour

*2 eggs

*1/2 tsp. vanilla extract

*1/4 cup sugar

*1/2 to 1 tsp. ground cinnamon

Directions:

1. Preheat 1 1/2 to 2 inches of vegetable oil in a 10 to 12 inch frying pan to 375 degrees F. In a separate dish mix the 1/4 cup sugar and cinnamon and set aside.

2. In a 3 qt. sauce pan add the water, brown sugar, salt, and butter and heat to a good boil. Remove from the heat and add the flour. Stirring in the flour will take some muscle. Mix it in until well blended.

3. In a separate bowl, mix the eggs and vanilla together and then add this mixture to the flour mixture. Stir until well blended and all the egg is completely mixed in.

4. Fill your decorating tool with the churro recipe dough and attach the largest star tip you have.

5. Test your oil by placing a small amount of dough in it. The dough should bubble up right away or that means the oil is not hot enough and a soggy churro is on the way.

6. Once the oil is hot enough, squeeze some dough (with decorator) into the oil about 4 inches long. I used my finger to release the dough from the decorator. Careful not to burn yourself.

7. You should be able to cook 4 or 5 churros at a time. Cook them about 1 minute and turn them over with a slotted spoon. Cook an additional minute or two. You're looking for that nice golden brown color.

8. Remove the churros with the slotted spoon and place them on a paper towel-covered plate to absorb excess grease.

9. While still warm, roll each churro into the dish with the sugar and cinnamon until coated.

Tips to help get started. I suggest trying out your cooking business with a focus group or test group. We chose to gather as many family members and friends with kids to come for a FREE cooking class. They ranged in ages 3-16yrs. old. This helped with learning how to manage all the 4C's. We also had the children and parents fill-out a feedback card to get more insight on how to improve our business, anonymously!

Test every recipe you plan to use, let a child taste-test it and don't be afraid to change things to suit your tastes or quantity.

Always have extra ingredients in case something gets dropped or more guests arrive than originally planned.

Finally, have fun doing what you love to do! Being an entrepreneur can be both scary and exciting at the same time. Stay focused on your goals, don't try and do everything on your own and take things one step at a time.

Best wishes on your endeavors,
Kathe Hamilton and Kery Jackson

One more bonus! Here's a sample of a Press Release to send out to newspapers and radio stations when you are ready to announce your business opening.

Coming Soon To
_____ " _____ "
Helping children to make healthy food choices in
_____ " _____ " is
mixing up fun recipes while integrating math, science, and language arts skills.

If you have a child who loves to cook or help out in the kitchen, then _____ is a great option for you. More importantly, they need to be at your next event or a part of your school curriculum or after school program. This premier health-oriented business was created by _____, who wanted to combine their passion for children and their love for cooking. With more than _____ years of experience as _____, they realized the growing need to have children make healthy food choices and learn valuable skills in the kitchen that will last them a lifetime. _____ has only been in existence for ____. However, they continuously receive accolades from students, parents, and educators about their engaging personalities and creative and healthy dishes.

There is no doubt that _____
mission is to provide a fun, creative and educational
cooking experience for children. They offer cooking
classes for kids' ages 4-16 years old, creative
nutrition lessons that make learning fun and themed
cooking parties.

Why _____ classes are
great for your child:

- Build self-esteem, independence
- Integrates math, science and language arts skills
- Improves fine motor skills and hand-eye coordination
- Improves listening and following directions
- Promotes cooperative learning and sharing
- Awareness of different cultures and traditions
- Encourages kids to make healthy food choices

For more information contact

_____

_____

About the Authors

<u>Kathe Hamilton, Co-Founder</u>

Kathe Hamilton holds a BS degree in Child Development from San Diego State University. and a Masters in Educational Administration from Concordia University, Irvine. She has been a credentialed teacher for over 24 years. While working in LAUSD she implemented the Nutrition Network program and taught Nutrition classes at the middle school level. She is a dedicated mother with a sincere love for educating children and is excited about the opportunity to combine this passion with the development of creative cooking experiences.

Kery Jackson, Co-Founder

Kery Jackson holds a BA in Psychology and a Masters in Educational Administration from UCLA. She has been a credentialed teacher and administrator in education for over 27 years. She has worked with the Nutrition Network through LAUSD, which strives to educate kids about health and nutrition. She is a dedicated mother with a passion for cooking and has taken several cooking classes under gourmet chefs in Los Angeles. Kids' Cooking Place is a way to fulfill a dream of combining her passion for cooking and a lifetime of experience educating children.

Printed in Great Britain
by Amazon